BIBLE STUDIES

D0330431

How Do You Walk the Walk You Talk?

Kay Arthur

PRECEPT MINISTRIES INTERNATIONAL

WATERBROOK
PRESS

How Do You Walk the Walk You Talk?
Published by WaterBrook Press
12265 Oracle Boulevard, Suite 200
Colorado Springs, Colorado 80921

All Scripture quotations, unless otherwise indicated, are taken from the New American Standard Bible® (NASB), © Copyright The Lockman Foundation 1960, 1962, 1963, 1968, 1971, 1972, 1973, 1975, 1977, 1995. Used by permission. (www.Lockman.org)

Italics in Scripture quotations reflect the author's added emphasis.

ISBN: 978-0-307-45763-9

Published in the United States by WaterBrook Multnomah, an imprint of the Crown Publishing Group, a division of Random House Inc., New York.

WATERBROOK and its deer colophon are registered trademarks of Random House Inc.

Printed in the United States of America
2012

10 9 8 7 6

Special Sales
Most WaterBrook Multnomah books are available at special quantity discounts when purchased in bulk by corporations, organizations, and special-interest groups. Custom imprinting or excerpting can also be done to fit special needs. For information, please e-mail SpecialMarkets@WaterBrookMultnomah.com or call 1-800-603-7051.

HOW TO USE THIS STUDY

This small-group study is for people who are interested in learning more about what the Bible says, but who have only limited time to meet together. It's ideal, for example, for a lunch group at work, an early morning men's group, a young mother's group meeting in a home, or a smaller Sunday-school class. (It's also ideal for small groups that typically have longer meeting times—such as evening groups or Saturday morning groups—but want to devote only a portion of their time together to actual study, while reserving the rest for prayer, fellowship, or other activities.)

This book is designed so that all the group's participants will complete each lesson's study activities *at the same time, while you're together.*

However, you'll need a facilitator to lead the group—someone to keep the discussion moving. (This person's function is *not* that of a lecturer or teacher. However, when this book is used in a Sunday-school class or similar setting, the teacher should feel free to lead more directly and to bring in other insights in addition to those provided in each week's lesson.)

If *you* are your group's facilitator, the leader, here are some helpful points for making your job easier:

- Go through the lesson and mark the text before you lead the group. This will give you increased familiarity with the material and will enable you to facilitate the group with greater ease. It may be easier for you to lead the group through the instructions for marking if you as a leader choose a specific color for each symbol you mark.

- As you lead the group, start at the beginning of the text and simply read it aloud in the order it appears in the lesson, including the "insight boxes," which may appear either before or after the instructions or in the midst of your observations or discussion. Work through the lesson together, observing and discussing what you learn. As you read the Scripture verses, have the group say aloud the word they are marking in the text.

- The discussion questions are there simply to help you cover the material. As the class moves into the discussion, many times you will find that they will cover the questions on their own. Remember the discussion questions are there to guide the group through the topic, not to squelch discussion.

- Remember how important it is for people to verbalize their answers and discoveries. This greatly strengthens their personal understanding of each week's lesson. Try to ensure that everyone has plenty of opportunity to contribute to each week's discussions.

- Keep the discussion moving. This may mean spending more time on some parts of the study than on others. If necessary, you should feel free to spread out a lesson over more than one session. However, remember that you don't want to slow the pace too much. It's much better to leave everyone "wanting more" than to have people dropping out because of declining interest.

- If the validity or accuracy of some of the answers seems questionable, you can gently and cheerfully remind the group to stay focused on the truth of the Scriptures. Your object is to learn what the Bible says, not to engage in human philosophy. Really *read* the Scriptures, asking God to show everyone His answers.

HOW DO YOU WALK THE WALK YOU TALK?

You've probably heard the expression "Words are cheap." Maybe someone said that to you when you made a promise—and they added, "Yeah, sure! We'll see."

And that is it! They *will* wait and see if your promise is really true, if it will really come to pass—if you're going to "walk the walk you talk."

This is what you're going to see for yourself while taking an inductive look at a few passages from the book of Ephesians. By *inductive* we mean that rather than simply listening to what others say about the subject, you're going to see for yourself what God says about the walk of a true believer in Jesus Christ.

DISCUSS

Leader: Have the group spend about ten minutes discussing the following questions. They may want to jot down their insights under each question or in the sidebar column.

Do you know people who talk about their Christianity and yet they really don't walk it—or at least not the way you think they ought to walk it? What causes you to wonder, to doubt?

How do you think Christians ought to walk in respect to...
    their relationship to God?

    their relationship to their mates, their family?

    their relationship to others?

    their relationship to their enemies?

What do you think their standards ought to be?

What about their morals?

What do you think a Christian's perspective on the Word of God, the Bible, ought to be? How would you describe what a Christian's relationship to the Bible should look like?

What are some of the things that you think keep people from being what they ought to be? From believing what the Word of God says about them?

OBSERVE

In two weeks we're going to take a close look in the Bible at the fourth and fifth chapters of Paul's letter to the Ephesians.

These chapters deal with walking the walk we talk as Christians.

In preparation for that time, we first need to take a look at ourselves from God's perspective. What does He say about those who are truly His children—those who believe on Jesus Christ and consequently receive Him as their Lord and Savior?

Leader: *Read Ephesians 1:1 aloud.*

DISCUSS

When you read the Word of God you need to train yourself to slow down long enough so that you really understand what God is saying. The Bible is the very Word of God, and it was written so that you might know truth and live by it.

This study will help you develop the inductive study skill of observation by interrogating the text with what we'll call the "five *W*s and an *H*"—who, what, when, where, why, and how. Let's try this approach on verse 1:

EPHESIANS 1:1

Paul, an apostle of Christ Jesus by the will of God, to the saints who are at Ephesus and who are faithful in Christ Jesus.

Who is writing? Who is he? How did he get to be that way?

To whom is he writing?

Where are they?

What are they called?

How are they described?

EPHESIANS 1:2-8a

2 Grace to you and peace from God our Father and the Lord Jesus Christ.

OBSERVE

*Leader: Read Ephesians 1:2-8a aloud. As you do, have the students follow you in the text and mark every occurrence of the words **we** and **us.** They can either color these words the same color or simply draw a circle around each occurrence.*

INSIGHT

The word *predestined* in the Greek language, the language of the New Testament, is *proorizo*. It comes from two words that, when combined, mean "to limit in advance," with the figurative meaning of "to predetermine." When this word is used, it's important to note *who* has been predestined and *to what*.

The word *redemption* in the Greek language is *apolutrosis* and refers to a releasing upon payment of a ransom. According to Ephesians 1:7, the ransom that released Christians from their sin was the blood of Jesus Christ.

3 Blessed be the God and Father of our Lord Jesus Christ, who has blessed us with every spiritual blessing in the heavenly places in Christ,

4 just as He chose us in Him before the foundation of the world, that we would be holy and blameless before Him. In love

5 He predestined us to adoption as sons through Jesus Christ to Himself, according to the kind intention of His will,

6 to the praise of the glory of His grace, which He freely bestowed on us in the Beloved.

7 In Him we have redemption through His blood, the forgiveness of our trespasses, according to the riches of His grace

8 which He lavished on us.

OBSERVE

*Leader: Have the students read through the passage again and this time mark every occurrence of the phrases **in Him, in Christ,** and **in the Beloved.** They can mark these phrases with a cloud like this:* ☁ *Also have them mark every occurrence of the phrase **according to** with a squiggly line like this:* ～～～～

DISCUSS

Beginning with verse 3, look at every *we* or *us* that you've circled and discuss point by point what you learn about *us* from observing the text. As you do, notice *where* those blessings are. Notice also the repeated phrase *according to.* What does this phrase connect?

Leader: If there's time, the students may want to list their observations in the sidebar column.

What do you think about what you've observed? How would you feel if you knew for certain that the things you marked were also true of *you?*

How does this compare with the way you normally see yourself?

WRAP IT UP

So often our behavior is dictated by the image, the perception we have of ourselves. What we believe about ourselves determines the way we "walk."

We'll look at these verses in greater depth next week, along with others that will help you see yourself from God's perspective. In the meantime, you might want to simply talk to God about what you've observed this week. In fact you may want to write Ephesians 1:3-8a on a card and read the verses aloud three times every morning, then three times again at noon, and finally three more times just before you go to bed. This should make for a better day—and sweet dreams!

Have you ever stopped to consider just how much God loves you—and what that love motivated God to do for you?

If you watch people carefully you'll see a noticeable difference between the behavior of those who know they're loved and the behavior of those who don't feel loved by anyone, let alone God.

As Paul writes to the believers living in Ephesus, before he ever discusses with them how they're to walk, he first makes sure they know how God views them and what His purpose is for them not only collectively but individually.

OBSERVE

Leader: *Read Ephesians 1:3-14 and have the students mark the text according to these instructions:*

*Circle or color each occurrence of the words **we, us, you,** and (**your.**) ("You" and "your" appear first in verse 13.)*

Put a cloud around every occurrence of the phrase **in Him.**

Put a squiggly line under every occurrence of the phrase **according to.**

Put a heart over every mention of the word **love**.

Although the group read and marked Ephesians 1:3-8 last week, you'll want to mark those verses again along with those that follow.

EPHESIANS 1:3-14

3 Blessed be the God and Father of our Lord Jesus Christ, who has blessed us with every spiritual blessing in the heavenly places in Christ,

4 just as He chose us in Him before the foundation of the world, that we would be holy and blameless before Him. In love

5 He predestined us to adoption as sons through Jesus Christ to Himself, according to the kind intention of His will,

6 to the praise of the glory of His grace, which He freely bestowed on us in the Beloved.

7 In Him we have redemption through His blood, the forgiveness of our trespasses, according to the riches of His grace

8 which He lavished on us. In all wisdom and insight

INSIGHT

The Greek word for *grace* is *charis*. It means "favor." When we talk of the grace of God and summarize the way God uses it in His Word in reference to our salvation, grace is often defined as "unmerited favor"—that which cannot be earned in any way for any reason. Grace is something God freely, lavishly bestows upon sinners who believe in His Son, the Lord Jesus Christ.

DISCUSS

There are abundant treasures of truth in these verses (including many we won't have time to explore). They give us a taste of the greatness of the love with which God has loved us. And we don't want to miss what He has for those who believe Him and who live accordingly.

Discuss what you learn from marking the words *we, us, you,* and *your* in verses

8-14. What do we have in Christ? You may want to briefly list your insights and those shared by other students in the space below.

OBSERVE

Mark all references to the **Holy Spirit,** including the pronoun *who,* with a symbol like this:

DISCUSS

What do you learn about the Holy Spirit from Ephesians 1:13-14?

What is the progression of events in Ephesians 1:13-14?

9 He made known to us the mystery of His will, according to His kind intention which He purposed in Him

10 with a view to an administration suitable to the fullness of the times, that is, the summing up of all things in Christ, things in the heavens and things on the earth. In Him

11 also we have obtained an inheritance, having been predestined according to His purpose who works all things after the counsel of His will,

12 to the end that we who were the first to hope in Christ would be to the praise of His glory.

13 In Him, you also, after listening to the message of truth, the gospel of your salvation—having also believed, you were sealed in Him with the Holy Spirit of promise,

14 who is given as a pledge of our inheritance, with a view to the redemption of God's own possession, to the praise of His glory.

INSIGHT

When Paul says the Holy Spirit "is given as a pledge of our inheritance," he means that the indwelling Holy Spirit is a guarantee that upon physical death we'll be taken to heaven and someday receive a brand-new immortal, incorruptible body (1 Corinthians 15:51-54).

OBSERVE

When did God first love us and choose us? Was it when we finally believed on His Son, the Lord Jesus Christ, and when we got rid of our sin, our shame?

Leader: *Read Ephesians 2:1-10. Once again have the students color or draw a circle around every occurrence of the words* **you,** **we,** *and* **us**—*every reference to* **Paul** *and to the* **recipients** *whom he includes with himself. Also put a heart over every occurrence of the word* **love** *and a cloud around every occurrence of the phrases* **in Him, with Him,** *and* **in Christ Jesus.**

DISCUSS

What do you learn from marking every reference to *you, we,* and *us?*

Leader: *Don't spend too long discussing the observations in Ephesians 2:1-3, as you'll look at those verses more thoroughly in the weeks to come. Make sure you cover verses 4-10.*

EPHESIANS 2:1-10

¹ And you were dead in your trespasses and sins,

² in which you formerly walked according to the course of this world, according to the prince of the power of the air, of the spirit that is now working in the sons of disobedience.

³ Among them we too all formerly lived in the lusts of our flesh, indulging the desires of the flesh and of the mind, and were by nature children of wrath, even as the rest.

4 But God, being rich in mercy, because of His great love with which He loved us,

5 even when we were dead in our transgressions, made us alive together with Christ (by grace you have been saved),

6 and raised us up with Him, and seated us with Him in the heavenly places in Christ Jesus,

7 so that in the ages to come He might show the surpassing riches of His grace in kindness toward us in Christ Jesus.

8 For by grace you have been saved through faith; and that not of yourselves, it is the gift of God;

What do you learn about God from Ephesians 2:4-6?

According to the verses you just read from the Word of God, *when* did God love you?

For all people whom God has saved, what state were they in when He saved them?

On what basis did God save them? What does this negate on our part?

According to Ephesians 2:10, where were we created and what were we created for? Who determines what these are?

Finally, what would happen in your life if you fully believed all you've seen these past two weeks—*really* believed, no matter what you felt, no matter what others said about you? How secure do you think you would be? How do you think it would affect your walk?

9 not as a result of works, so that no one may boast.

10 For we are His workmanship, created in Christ Jesus for good works, which God prepared beforehand so that we would walk in them.

WRAP IT UP

Once again, why don't you continue reading Ephesians 2:1-10 aloud at three different points in your day (three times through each time). Begin your day with these truths, and let them be the last ones on your mind as you go to sleep.

Talk to this one and only God who loves you with an incomprehensible love, who offers you His extravagant, lavish grace right where you are.

Next week we'll look at the way our heavenly Father expects His children to walk.

OBSERVE

In the first three chapters of Ephesians, Paul reminds "the saints who are at Ephesus" of their position in Christ. Now his letter takes a turn from doctrine to duty, from position to performance.

How are those who have been saved by grace to live? Does grace give us license to live any way we want? Or does it give us the power to walk as we ought to walk? How crucial is it that our walk matches our talk if we bear the name "Christian"? And what if it doesn't?

Leader: Read aloud the verses shown from Ephesians 4:1,17; 5:1-2,8,15. Have the group watch for a key repeated word that will show you what these two chapters in Ephesians are about.

EPHESIANS 4:1

Therefore I, the prisoner of the Lord, implore you to walk in a manner worthy of the calling with which you have been called.

EPHESIANS 4:17

So this I say, and affirm together with the Lord, that you walk no longer just as the Gentiles also walk, in the futility of their mind.

EPHESIANS 5:1-2

¹ Therefore be imitators of God, as beloved children;

² and walk in love, just as Christ also loved you and gave Himself up for us, an offering and a sacrifice to God as a fragrant aroma.

EPHESIANS 5:8

For you were formerly darkness, but now you are Light in the Lord; walk as children of Light.

EPHESIANS 5:15

Therefore be careful how you walk, not as unwise men but as wise.

Now what is the key repeated word in each passage?

Draw a cloud like this around each occurrence:

What do you learn from observing this key word?

Having told the Ephesians *who they are in Christ* (in the first three chapters of this letter), Paul now begins his practical exhortations to them (and to us as well).

Leader: Read through Ephesians 4:1-6. Have the students either color code or circle every reference to the **Ephesians,** the recipients of this letter. As the students mark each appropriate word, have them say it aloud as you come to it in the text. That way everyone will make sure to mark every reference.

DISCUSS

Now that you've marked in this passage the references to this letter's recipients, what do you observe that Paul is entreating the people to do?

OBSERVE

Mark what Paul is entreating the believers to do in verse 1 by putting a cloud around it.

EPHESIANS 4:1-6

1 Therefore I, the prisoner of the Lord, implore you to walk in a manner worthy of the calling with which you have been called,

2 with all humility and gentleness, with patience, showing tolerance for one another in love,

3 being diligent to preserve the unity of the Spirit in the bond of peace.

⁴ There is one body and one Spirit, just as also you were called in one hope of your calling;

⁵ one Lord, one faith, one baptism,

⁶ one God and Father of all who is over all and through all and in all.

DISCUSS

Now that you've identified what Paul is entreating them to do in verse 1, discuss this question: *How* are they to do it? Take a few minutes to talk about how this is answered in verses 2-3, where we see the different qualities and attitudes that are to be evident in their lives. You can number each of these in the text. (See the example with "humility" in verse 2.)

OBSERVE

In verses 4-6, underline each occurrence of the word *one.*

DISCUSS

According to verses 4-6, what is the basis of their unity—what do all believers hold in common?

OBSERVE

Having reminded the Ephesians in verses 4-6 of the unity of the Spirit and of the things that all true believers hold in common, Paul now turns to the diversity within the body.

*Leader: Read Ephesians 4:7-13. Once again, have the group color or circle every reference to the **recipients**. Make sure you mark the pronouns, including **we** or **us** where the author includes himself with the recipients.*

DISCUSS

NOTE: We will not discuss verses 9-10, which are a parenthetical teaching and not pertinent to the discussion of our topic. Time constraints do not permit it.

What do you learn from marking the recipients in verse 7?

EPHESIANS 4:7-13

7 But to each one of us grace was given according to the measure of Christ's gift.

8 Therefore it says, "When He ascended on high, He led captive a host of captives, and He gave gifts to men."

9 (Now this expression, "He ascended," what does it mean except that He also had descended into the lower parts of the earth?

10 He who descended is Himself also He who ascended far above all the heavens, so that He might fill all things.)

11 And He gave some as apostles, and some as prophets, and some as evangelists, and some as pastors and teachers,

12 for the equipping of the saints for the work of service, to the building up of the body of Christ;

13 until we all attain to the unity of the faith, and of the knowledge of the Son of God, to a mature man, to the measure of the stature which belongs to the fullness of Christ.

What are the diverse gifts (gifted men) given to the church, as mentioned by Paul in verse 11?

What is the purpose of these gifted men in the body? What do these men do?

Leader: Don't get in an extensive discussion of these gifts. Rather discuss how those who are given these gifts will benefit the saints.

INSIGHT

Saints (4:12) means "holy ones," those "set apart" because they now belong to God through salvation from their sins—a salvation that came through believing that Jesus Christ died for their sins as their substitute and rose from the dead three days later.

Equipping (also in 4:12) is the translation of a Greek word used in New Testament times for mending nets, setting a bone, and realizing a purpose. It means to "put right."

OBSERVE

In Ephesians 4:3 we saw the phrase **the unity of the Spirit,** while in verse 13 we see a reference to **the unity of the faith.** Put a large box around these two phrases or color them in a distinctive way.

DISCUSS

What is the difference between the two? What did you see when you marked these two phrases: *the unity of the Spirit* and *the unity of the faith*? What is our responsibility to each one?

According to verse 13, to what else are we all to attain in order to become mature?

Also according to this verse, what does "a mature man" look like? To what or whom is he to measure up?

Ask yourself how you measure up to this description of maturity. Just from these first thirteen verses, is there a way to know if we're maturing? Are these attributes increasing in your life?

EPHESIANS 4:14-16

14 As a result, we are no longer to be children, tossed here and there by waves and carried about by every wind of doctrine, by the trickery of men, by craftiness in deceitful scheming;

15 but speaking the truth in love, we are to grow up in all aspects into Him who is the head, even Christ,

16 from whom the whole body, being fitted and held together by what every joint supplies, according to the proper working of each individual part, causes the growth of the body for the building up of itself in love.

OBSERVE

How does a person attain maturity? Read Ephesians 4:14-16 and watch for words that show how this happens. Once more, mark each reference to the letter's **recipients.**

DISCUSS

According to verse 14 we are no longer to be _____ (fill in the blank). How are they further described in this verse? What do you think it means to be "tossed here and there"?

How and where do you see immaturity among believers today? Do you know people like that?

Where is truth to be found? In John 17:17, Jesus prays to the Father, "Sanctify them in the truth; Your word is truth." In Ephesians 4:15 mark **truth** like this: ▱▱

According to verse 15, what is the answer to immaturity?

If we grow up into Christ, how does this parallel with verse 13?

OBSERVE

Leader: Read verse 16 again. Call attention to the phrase "according to the proper working of each individual part."

According to this verse, when all the parts of the body of Christ—all true believers— are working together as a body, attaining the unity of the faith, and being ministered to by gifted men who are equipping them, then the body is going to grow and we will see the church building itself up in love.

The word **love** is a key repeated word in Ephesians 4. Find each occurrence of this word in verses 2, 15, and 16, and draw a heart around it, like this:

DISCUSS

What do you learn from these verses? How do you love? What should be your motive? How do you speak the truth in love? How does the body build itself up in love?

WRAP IT UP

If a person is going to walk in a manner worthy of his calling as a Christian—or to put it another way, if a person claims to be a Christian and wants to walk his talk—what would he need to do, according to what you've seen in today's study?

If all believers did this, what would this do for the body of Christ collectively?

Are you maturing and doing your part in the body of Christ, or are you one of those people who are "tossed here and there" (4:14)? To avoid this experience, what do you need to do—or keep doing?

Last week we saw that we are to walk in a manner worthy of the calling to which we have been called as children of God (Ephesians 4:1).

And what is our goal? It is to "preserve [or keep] the unity of the Spirit in the bond of peace," all the while realizing that God is in the process of "building up the body of Christ until we all attain to the unity of the faith, and of the knowledge of the Son of God."

The goal is *maturity.* Christlikeness. And it is achieved by growing up.

Growth comes when every member of the body operates as he or she should. To do this, we need to speak the truth. "Speaking" the truth could also be translated as "holding to" or "walking in" the truth of God's Word. And this is to be done "in love." That's why you're doing this study—so you can discover truth for yourself and thus walk and talk accordingly.

This week we want to see how genuine Christianity affects a person's morals and his or her interpersonal relationships. In these areas, should there be a noticeable difference between the walk of the person who professes to know God and the life of someone who doesn't know Him?

OBSERVE

Leader: *Read Ephesians 4:17-21. As you did last week, each student should follow along in the text and circle every reference to the* **recipients** *of this letter—the words* **you** *and* **your.**

EPHESIANS 4:17-21

17 So this I say, and affirm together with the Lord, that you walk no longer just as the Gentiles also walk, in the futility of their mind,

18 being darkened in their understanding, excluded from the life of God because of the ignorance that is in them, because of the hardness of their heart;

19 and they, having become callous, have given themselves over to sensuality for the practice of every kind of impurity with greediness.

20 But you did not learn Christ in this way,

21 if indeed you have heard Him and have been taught in Him, just as truth is in Jesus.

INSIGHT

Sensuality in verse 19 means license in the sphere of the physical and thus indicates debauchery. It often refers to sexual excesses and the lack of restraints.

DISCUSS

According to these verses **how** are believers to walk? (Mark it with a cloud.) What does 4:17 say?

Who is contrasted with whom in verses 17-20, and what do you learn about each? Obviously one group is described in more detail than the other. Discuss what the text tells you about this group. What are they like? Does this sound like today? Should this describe Christians? How do you know?

OBSERVE

Leader: *Read verses 20-21 and mark every reference to* **Christ** *with a cross, along with any names or pronouns that refer to Him.*

DISCUSS

What do you learn about Christ from marking these verses?

If you want truth, where should you go?

OBSERVE

Leader: *Read Ephesians 4:20-24, which appears on page 32, while the students underline the phrases* **old/self** *(literally, "old man") and* **new self** *(literally, "new man"), plus all the references to the letter's* **recipients.**

EPHESIANS 4:20-24

20 But you did not learn Christ in this way,

21 if indeed you have heard Him and have been taught in Him, just as truth is in Jesus,

22 that, in reference to your former manner of life, you lay aside the old self, which is being corrupted in accordance with the lusts of deceit,

23 and that you be renewed in the spirit of your mind,

24 and put on the new self, which in the likeness of God has been created in righteousness and holiness of the truth.

INSIGHT

The terms *old self* and *new self* (old man and new man) are used in only two other passages—Colossians 3:9-11 and Romans 6:1-7. When you study Ephesians 4:22-24 together with these, you see that the death of the old man is something that was effected with our identification in Christ at the time of our salvation. Now we are to live in the light of this change—as a new creation in Christ Jesus (2 Corinthians 5:17).

DISCUSS

What do you learn from Ephesians 4:22-24 about the old self and about the new self?

Do you see anything about the old self that parallels what you have seen in the "Gentiles" who do not know God (as mentioned in verses 17-19)?

What does verse 24 tell us about how the new self is created?

In verse 21 we read that the "truth is in Jesus." How do verses 22-24 further explain this? (Watch how the word *that* in verses 22-23 and the phrase *and put* in verse 24 lead you to see what is the truth in Jesus.)

How are you renewed in the spirit of your mind?

OBSERVE

*Leader: Read Ephesians 4:25-32, while the students circle every reference to the **recipients**, including the pronoun **we**.*

INSIGHT

The word translated as *unwholesome* in verse 29 means "bad, rotten, putrid." Figuratively, in a moral sense, it means "corrupt, foul."

EPHESIANS 4:25-32

25 Therefore, laying aside falsehood, speak truth each one of you with his neighbor, for we are members of one another.

26 Be angry, and yet do not sin; do not let the sun go down on your anger,

27 and do not give the devil an opportunity.

28 He who steals must steal no longer; but rather he must labor, performing with his own hands what is good, so that he will have something to share with one who has need.

29 Let no unwholesome word proceed from your mouth, but only such a word as is good for edification according to the need of the moment, so that it will give grace to those who hear.

30 Do not grieve the Holy Spirit of God, by whom you were sealed for the day of redemption.

31 Let all bitterness and wrath and anger and clamor and slander be put away from you, along with all malice.

32 Be kind to one another, tender-hearted, forgiving each other, just as God in Christ also has forgiven you.

DISCUSS

Leader: Read through Ephesians 4:25-32 again. As you read, note the instructions given in each verse and discuss them verse by verse. Talk about how each instruction applies to us today. Also note which part of the instructions fits the old self and which part fits the new self.

According to verse 27, what will happen if you stay angry, if you dwell on the anger?

Why should we labor, according to verse 28?

What does verse 29 tell us should come from our mouths?

How could we grieve the Holy Spirit? Why would such actions grieve Him? (Consider whether these are characteristic of the old self or new self.)

Is there anyone you have not forgiven?

When you come to the instructions in verse 32, note the comparison given in regard to forgiving. Why are we to forgive? Why don't we?

OBSERVE

*Leader: Have the group read verse 30 again aloud. Then mark the reference to the **Spirit**, along with the pronoun **whom**, since it is a pronoun for the Spirit. Mark it like this:*

⌒ Spirit ⌒

Then read Ephesians 4:3-4 while the group marks each reference to the Spirit in these verses.

DISCUSS

Discuss what you learn about yourself as a believer and about the Spirit in these verses.

From all you have learned, what do you think would "grieve" the Spirit of God— something we're told in Ephesians 4:30 to avoid doing?

EPHESIANS 4:3-4

3 being diligent to preserve the unity of the Spirit in the bond of peace.

4 There is one body and one Spirit, just as also you were called in one hope of your calling.

WRAP IT UP

Read Ephesians 4:17 again. According to this week's study, what did you learn about walking your walk?

Finally, is your walk any different since you believed in Jesus Christ and identified yourself as a Christian? Is there a new self? Is your lifestyle different because of Christ? If not, what could that mean?

As you saw last week in Ephesians 4:1, you're to walk in a manner worthy of your calling. What have you seen in this lesson that relates to that?

Last week we saw that we are no longer to walk like the Gentiles walk. We have put on the new self. Now we are to walk according to the truth that is in Jesus Christ.

Have you ever talked with someone who claimed to be a Christian and yet lived in a way that is contrary to the commandments of God? He is sure that he would go to heaven if he died because he's made a "profession" of faith, yet he lives just like the world lives! What does God say about this? Can a person walk in the darkness when he claims to belong to the Light of the World, the Lord Jesus Christ?

OBSERVE

Leader: Read Ephesians 5:1-6, reprinted in the sidebars on pages 37-38. Mark every reference to the letter's recipients, as you've done previously. Also mark the word love with a heart and put a cloud around the phrase that tells you how you are to walk.

DISCUSS

According to Ephesians 5:1-2, how are believers to walk? To what degree of love? What is the comparison in verse 2?

EPHESIANS 5:1-6

1 Therefore be imitators of God, as beloved children;

2 and walk in love, just as Christ also loved you and gave Himself up for us, an offering and a sacrifice to God as a fragrant aroma.

3 But immorality or any impurity or greed must not even be named among you, as is proper among saints;

4 and there must be no filthiness and silly talk, or coarse jesting, which are not fitting, but rather giving of thanks.

5 For this you know with certainty, that no immoral or impure person or covetous man, who is an idolater, has an inheritance in the kingdom of Christ and God.

6 Let no one deceive you with empty words, for because of these things the wrath of God comes upon the sons of disobedience.

Is this kind of walk easy or difficult? Why?

OBSERVE

Leader: *Read verses 3-4 aloud. If the class did not circle the word **saints** when they marked the recipients, they should do so now. ("Saints" could also be translated as "holy ones." It is a term used by God to refer to all genuine Christians.)*

DISCUSS

What is not to be named among the saints, according to 5:3-4? Go over the list and discuss how these things would keep you from being an imitator of God and from walking in love.

What is to be done by the saints instead?

OBSERVE

*Leader: Read Ephesians 5:5-6 again, reprinted for you here in the sidebar. Have the group double underline, preferably in red, the phrases **for this you know with certainty** and **Let no one deceive you with empty words.***

DISCUSS

What are the believers admonished to know? What should they not be deceived about?

How are they not to be deceived?

EPHESIANS 5:5-6

5 For this you know with certainty, that no immoral or impure person or covetous man, who is an idolater, has an inheritance in the kingdom of Christ and God.

6 Let no one deceive you with empty words, for because of these things the wrath of God comes upon the sons of disobedience.

INSIGHT

In Ephesians 5:6, *empty* means "void of truth, of reality." It indicates the hollowness of something or somebody.

What do you think God means by "empty words"? Deceived about what? Could it be that they were being told that they could be a Christian and live like this?

Does this happen today? What is the warning for us? What can we know if there is no life change?

1 CORINTHIANS 6:9-11

⁹ Or do you not know that the unrighteous will not inherit the kingdom of God? Do not be deceived; neither fornicators, nor idolaters, nor adulterers, nor effeminate, nor homosexuals,

¹⁰ nor thieves, nor the covetous, nor drunkards, nor revilers, nor swindlers, will inherit the kingdom of God.

OBSERVE

*Leader: Read aloud 1 Corinthians 6:9-11. Watch for the admonition **Do not be deceived** and double underline it.*

DISCUSS

Why the warning not to be deceived? Is it possible for a Christian to be deceived? What had we better do?

According to this passage in 1 Corinthians 6, what are they not to be deceived about?

According to these verses in 1 Corinthians 6, who will *not* inherit the kingdom of God?

Were the Corinthian believers ever like what is described in verses 9-10? According to verse 11, what had happened to them?

OBSERVE

According to Ephesians 5:6, how are the people (mentioned in verse 5) described?

Leader: Read Ephesians 2:1-3. Have the students mark the words formerly and walked. Also mark the phrases **sons of disobedience** *and* **children of wrath** *in the same way.*

DISCUSS

What do you learn from marking the word *formerly*? What does the word *formerly* tell us? How did the Ephesian believers formerly "walk" (live)? How are they described? Why?

11 Such were some of you; but you were washed, but you were sanctified, but you were justified in the name of the Lord Jesus Christ and in the Spirit of our God.

EPHESIANS 2:1-3

1 And you were dead in your trespasses and sins,

2 in which you formerly walked according to the course of this world, according to the prince of the power of the air, of the spirit that is now working in the sons of disobedience.

3 Among them we too all formerly lived in the lusts of our flesh, indulging the desires of the flesh and of the mind, and were by nature children of wrath, even as the rest.

Did you notice the occurrence of the word *wrath* in Ephesians 2:1-3 and 5:6? What connection do you see between these two usages of the word?

EPHESIANS 5:6-14

6 Let no one deceive you with empty words, for because of these things the wrath of God comes upon the sons of disobedience.

7 Therefore do not be partakers with them;

8 for you were formerly darkness, but now you are Light in the Lord; walk as children of Light

OBSERVE

Leader: Read Ephesians 5:6-14 and have the students mark the recipients as before. Also have them mark the words formerly, darkness, and light.

DISCUSS

According to verses 7-9, what is to be your response to the sons of disobedience? Why?

How are the believers to walk according to verse 8? Why? (Draw a cloud around (how) they are to walk.) What is the contrast?

9 (for the fruit of the Light consists in all goodness and righteousness and truth),

10 trying to learn what is pleasing to the Lord.

How does walking this way manifest itself? What does it produce? What can others see?

11 Do not participate in the unfruitful deeds of darkness, but instead even expose them;

12 for it is disgraceful even to speak of the things which are done by them in secret.

What instructions are given with respect to the things of darkness?

13 But all things become visible when they are exposed by the light, for everything that becomes visible is light.

According to verse 10, what should be your goal as a believer? Why?

14 For this reason it says, "Awake, sleeper, and arise from the dead, and Christ will shine on you."

INSIGHT

The word *exposed* in Ephesians 5:11,13 means "to admonish, to reprove with conviction upon the offender."

Think about what you have seen in this week's study. How could it be practically lived out among believers? And what about in society?

WRAP IT UP

Answer the questions that follow, questions posed at the beginning of this week's study:

Have you ever talked with someone who claims to be a Christian and yet lives in a way that is contrary to the commandments of God? Someone who feels sure of going to heaven because of a "profession" of faith, yet who lives just like the world—the Gentiles!

Can a person continually walk in darkness while claiming to belong to the Light of the World, the Lord Jesus Christ? How do you know?

What would you say to such a person? What would you show them from what you have studied these last five weeks about the walk of a true believer?

Finally, ask yourself if you are a son of disobedience or a son of God. How do you know? Do you walk your talk? Are you trying to find out what pleases the Lord?

We have seen that every genuine believer, every saint, is sealed by the Holy Spirit, and that the Holy Spirit is the guarantee that he or she is going to inherit heaven, eternal life.

We have also seen that the way a person knows he is a genuine Christian is that his walk matches his talk. He doesn't walk or live as he formerly lived—as the rest of the world lives. The old self has been dealt with. The new self has been put on. He no longer walks in darkness. He is a child of the light and walks as such.

But now the question comes: If a person has the Spirit living within, what should be his relationship with the Spirit, and how will this be manifested in his relationships with other people as well as inwardly?

OBSERVE

Leader: Read Ephesians 5:15-21. As the leader reads, once again mark the references to the (recipients.) *Also put a cloud around the* {admonition} *in respect to the believer's walk.*

DISCUSS

What is the admonition regarding our walk in this passage? What is the contrast in verse 15?

EPHESIANS 5:15-21

15 Therefore be careful how you walk, not as unwise men but as wise,

16 making the most of your time, because the days are evil.

17 So then do not be foolish, but understand what the will of the Lord is.

18 And do not get drunk with wine, for that is dissipation, but be filled with the Spirit,

19 speaking to one another in psalms and hymns and spiritual songs, singing and making melody with your heart to the Lord;

20 always giving thanks for all things in the name of our Lord Jesus Christ to God, even the Father;

21 and be subject to one another in the fear of Christ.

Discuss the contrasts you see in verse 15.

According to verse 16, what is important for you to know about time?

What is the contrast in verse 18? If a person is drunk, what does it affect?

From verses 18-21, if a person were walking under the control of the Spirit, how would He manifest Himself? What would the person be doing?

INSIGHT

In verse 18, the verb translated as "be filled" is in the present tense, which implies continual or habitual action. It is also in the middle voice, which means the subject participates in the action of the verb. In other words, the Spirit wants to fill you and will do His part; however, you have a role to play—you are to obey this command. The imperative mood of the verb makes it a command.

Of these instructions given to us in Ephesians 5:19-21—speaking, singing and making melody, always giving thanks for all things, and being subject to one another in the fear of the Lord—which is the most difficult for you to understand and to do? Why?

EPHESIANS 5:22-24

22 Wives, be subject to your own husbands, as to the Lord.

23 For the husband is the head of the wife, as Christ also is the head of the church, He Himself being the Savior of the body.

24 But as the church is subject to Christ, so also the wives ought to be to their husbands in everything.

OBSERVE

Leader: *Read Ephesians 5:22-24. Have the group follow along and mark every reference to **wives** and **husbands**—each in its own distinctive color or way—along with their pronouns. They can mark them like this:* ♀ *And this:* ♂ *Also put a box around each occurrence of the word* [as.]

INSIGHT

The Greek word translated as *subject* in Ephesians 5 is *hupotasso*. It's a military term and means "to rank under, to place under in an orderly fashion."

In this context the word is a present active imperative verb, therefore meaning that the wife does the subjecting—it is her responsibility to obey this command; it is not the husband's responsibility to force the subjection. The wife must choose to obey. Since it is in the present tense, this is to be a habitual or continuous action.

DISCUSS

What do you learn about the role of the wife in this passage? What is she to do in respect to her husband? What is her relationship to her husband?

What do you learn about the husband from verses 22-24? Discuss who the husband is compared to and how. What is Christ to the church?

According to verses 22 and 24, to what degree is the wife to subject herself to her husband? Are there any limits to this subjection? (If you have problems answering this, look at verse 22.)

Would the fact that the husband is likened to Christ, who is the Savior of the body (the church), help a wife understand in any way the parameters of her subjection to her husband? If he should ask her to do something against the Word of God or something that would hurt her or cause her to sin, should she do it? If your answer is no, please explain.

OBSERVE

*Leader: Read Ephesians 5:25-27 and have the group mark every occurrence of the words **husbands** and **wives**. Also mark the word **love** with a heart as you have before, and put a box around the word **as**.*

EPHESIANS 5:25-27

25 Husbands, love your wives, just as Christ also loved the church and gave Himself up for her,

26 so that He might sanctify her, having cleansed her by the washing of water with the word,

27 that He might present to Himself the church in all her glory, having no spot or wrinkle or any such thing; but that she would be holy and blameless.

INSIGHT

In Ephesians 5:25, the word translated as *love* is also a present active imperative verb (the same tense as the verb "be subject" that we looked at earlier). Therefore the husband is commanded to habitually love his wife. The responsibility to do so rests on him, not on the wife.

DISCUSS

What is the husband's responsibility to his wife?

Who is the husband's role model for his behavior toward his wife?

What did Christ do for the church, as mentioned in verses 25-26? And why did He do this, according to verse 27?

What does this tell you about the responsibility of the husband toward his wife? What is to be his goal, his mission for his wife? How is it to be carried out?

EPHESIANS 5:28-33

28 So husbands ought also to love their own wives as their own bodies. He who loves his own wife loves himself;

29 for no one ever hated his own flesh, but nourishes and cherishes it, just as Christ also does the church,

30 because we are members of His body.

31 For this reason a man shall leave his father and mother and shall be joined to his wife, and the two shall become one flesh.

32 This mystery is great; but I am speaking with reference to Christ and the church.

OBSERVE

Leader: Read Ephesians 5:28-33 while the group once again marks the references to **husbands** *and* **wives**. *Also mark the words* **love** *and* **as.**

INSIGHT

The words translated as *nourish* and *cherish* are both present tense, thereby implying continuous or habitual action. To nourish means "to rear, feed, bring to maturity." To cherish means "to make warm, to heat as a mother hen would do with her chicks under her wings."

DISCUSS

What do you learn from these verses about the husband's relationship to his wife? (Don't miss a thing.)

You may have covered it, but review it again: The husband is commanded to love his wife in two ways. This is seen in the phrases "just as" and "as." What are these two ways? (See verses 25 and 28.)

33 Nevertheless, each individual among you also is to love his own wife even as himself, and the wife must see to it that she respects her husband.

According to Ephesians 5:22 and 5:33, what is the wife told to do in respect to her husband? How do you think this would be lived out?

Having read this passage, who do you think has the greater task before God—the husband or the wife? Why?

When teaching or sharing the role of the wife in Ephesians 5:22-24, do you think it would be wise to always include the role of the husband in verses 25-33? Why or why not?

WRAP IT UP

Leader: *Have the group discuss how the Lord has spoken to them in this week's lesson.*

What is the most significant thing you have learned in these past six weeks? How has it already begun to affect the way you walk?

Leader: *Look again at the exhortations (from Ephesians 4:1,17 and 5:1-2,8,15) regarding the walk of the believer as listed at the beginning of Week Three's study. If there is time, review the essence of each exhortation and how it can be lived out.*

Finally, what have you learned about how to discern between the true and the false when it comes to Christianity—or do we have to wait until heaven to find out?

What have you learned from this study about the genuineness of your relationship with Jesus Christ? Is your faith real or not?

———

Well done! We're impressed. What a joy to encounter people like you who want to know truth for themselves and will take the time to learn!

From Your precepts I get understanding;
Therefore I hate every false way.

PSALM 119:104

40 MINUTE BIBLE STUDIES

No-Homework
That Help You

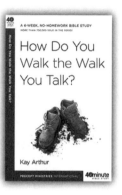

A 6-WEEK, NO-HOMEWORK BIBLE STUDY
MORE THAN 700,000 SOLD IN THE SERIES

Being a Disciple:
Counting the
Real Cost

Kay Arthur, Tom & Jane Hart

PRECEPT MINISTRIES INTERNATIONAL

40 minute BIBLE STUDY

A 6-WEEK, NO-HOMEWORK BIBLE STUDY
MORE THAN 700,000 SOLD IN THE SERIES

Having a Real
Relationship
with God

Kay Arthur

PRECEPT MINISTRIES INTERNATIONAL

40 minute BIBLE STUDY

A 6-WEEK, NO-HOMEWORK BIBLE STUDY
MORE THAN 700,000 SOLD IN THE SERIES

How Do You
Walk the Walk
You Talk?

Kay Arthur

PRECEPT MINISTRIES INTERNATIONAL

A 6-WEEK, NO-HOMEWORK BIBLE STUDY
MORE THAN 700,000 SOLD IN THE SERIES

Living a
Life of
True Worship

Kay Arthur, Bob & Diane Vereen

PRECEPT MINISTRIES INTERNATIONAL

40 minute BIBLE STUDY

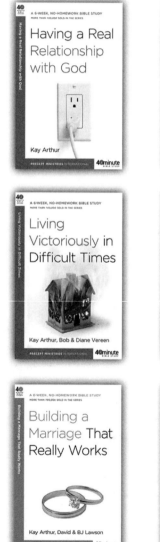

A 6-WEEK, NO-HOMEWORK BIBLE STUDY
MORE THAN 700,000 SOLD IN THE SERIES

Living
Victoriously in
Difficult Times

Kay Arthur, Bob & Diane Vereen

PRECEPT MINISTRIES INTERNATIONAL

40 minute BIBLE STUDY

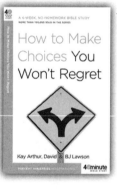

A 6-WEEK, NO-HOMEWORK BIBLE STUDY
MORE THAN 700,000 SOLD IN THE SERIES

How to Make
Choices You
Won't Regret

Kay Arthur, David & BJ Lawson

PRECEPT MINISTRIES INTERNATIONAL

40 minute BIBLE STUDY

A 6-WEEK, NO-HOMEWORK BIBLE STUDY
MORE THAN 700,000 SOLD IN THE SERIES

Money and
Possessions:
The Quest for
Contentment

Kay Arthur & David Arthur

PRECEPT MINISTRIES INTERNATIONAL

40 minute BIBLE STUDY

A 6-WEEK, NO-HOMEWORK BIBLE STUDY
MORE THAN 700,000 SOLD IN THE SERIES

Building a
Marriage That
Really Works

Kay Arthur, David & BJ Lawson

PRECEPT MINISTRIES INTERNATIONAL

40 minute BIBLE STUDY

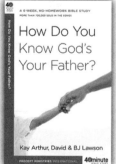

A 6-WEEK, NO-HOMEWORK BIBLE STUDY
MORE THAN 700,000 SOLD IN THE SERIES

How Do You
Know God's
Your Father?

Kay Arthur, David & BJ Lawson

PRECEPT MINISTRIES INTERNATIONAL

40 minute BIBLE STUDY

Bible Studies
Discover Truth For Yourself

A 6-WEEK, NO-HOMEWORK BIBLE STUDY

Discovering What the Future Holds

Kay Arthur & Georg Huber

A 6-WEEK, NO-HOMEWORK BIBLE STUDY
MORE THAN 700,000 SOLD IN THE SERIES

Forgiveness: Breaking the Power of the Past

Kay Arthur, David & BJ Lawson

A 6-WEEK, NO-HOMEWORK BIBLE STUDY

Living Like You Belong to God

Kay Arthur, David & BJ Lawson

A 6-WEEK, NO-HOMEWORK BIBLE STUDY

The Essentials of Effective Prayer

Kay Arthur, David & BJ Lawson

A 6-WEEK, NO-HOMEWORK BIBLE STUDY
MORE THAN 700,000 SOLD IN THE SERIES

Loving God and Others: The Heart of True Faith

Kay Arthur, David & BJ Lawson

A 6-WEEK, NO-HOMEWORK BIBLE STUDY
MORE THAN 700,000 SOLD IN THE SERIES

Understanding Spiritual Gifts

Kay Arthur, David and BJ Lawson

Also Available:
A Man's Strategy for Conquering Temptation
Rising to the Call of Leadership
Key Principles of Biblical Fasting
What Does the Bible Say About Sex?
Turning Your Heart Toward God
Fatal Distractions: Conquering Destructive Temptations
Spiritual Warfare: Overcoming the Enemy
The Power of Knowing God
Breaking Free from Fear